# Attributes
# to
# **Great**
# **Destiny**

Abel Jimmy

ISBN 979-8-89526-478-2 (paperback)
ISBN 979-8-89526-479-9 (digital)



Christian Faith Publishing
832 Park Avenue
Meadville, PA 16335
www.christianfaithpublishing.com

Printed in the United States of America

# Introduction

As a child of God, you have a great destiny in spite of the negative situations surrounding your life temporarily. God told Jeremiah that before He placed him on the earth, He had a great plan for him. Your destiny was preordained by God before He formed you in your mother's womb. What you will ever be in the future as a child of God, you are already. The Lord said to Abraham, "I have made you a father of many nations," while his wife, Sarai, was still barren (Genesis 17:5). What the Lord also meant when He promised Abraham is that He had already made him great when nothing around his life seemed great or situations were not in his favor.

Remember, as a child of God, we are the seed of Abraham and have the same destiny as Father Abraham. There is nothing God will make out of our lives that He hasn't placed inside us or made us already. What I want to draw your attention to in this book is that there are six attributes (contributors) that will fulfill the great destiny God has for you, which I'm going to explain in detail.

Speaking to Jeremiah, the Lord said, "For I know the plans I have for you," declares the Lord, "plans to prosper you and not to harm you, plans to give you hope and a future" (Jeremiah 29:11).

Anything that is evil or harmful is not God's plan or the destiny God has for you. The plan and purpose of God for you are good, and that is a great destiny.

However, for that greatness to be manifested in the physical, you must follow these six principles: divine timing, divine direction, faith, prayer, patience, and consecration. You may be wondering why all the promises of God for your life in His Word are not seen in your life. Or you may have a lot of questions in your mind about why another child of God is making progress in their walk with God, ministry, career, business, etc., while everything in your life is stagnant.

I believe that when you are through reading this book, it will answer most of your questions and guide you into the glorious destiny God has for you. You are too precious to our Lord Jesus Christ, and so is your destiny. It is frustrating to hear about your promised land that flows with milk and honey but not know how to enter it. I pray that the Holy Spirit enlightens your spirit to understand and follow the six attributes to actualizing destiny. Destiny is a process, and every process is guided by principles. Following the divine principles will remove the curtain covering the divine destiny God has for you.

> Your beginnings will seem humble, so prosperous will your future be. (Job 8:7 NIV)

# Chapter 1

# Divine Timing

*I will stand upon my watch, and set me upon the tower, and will watch to see what he will say unto me, and what I shall answer when I am reproved. And the* Lord *answered me, and said, Write the vision, and make it plain upon tables, that he may run that readeth it.* For the vision is yet for an appointed time, *but at the end it shall speak, and not lie: though it tarry, wait for it; because it will surely come, it will not tarry.*

—Habakkuk 2:1–3; reverse italics added

The spine of every great destiny in the kingdom is divine timing. The Lord honors times and seasons; that's why He has an appointed time for the fulfillment of every destiny. The Lord made His vision clear to Habakkuk but also told him that the vision was for an appointed time to be fulfilled. The Lord does not change. It's a great privilege being a child of God, but there is a great destiny the Lord has for you. I want you to be aware that the great plan and purpose the Lord has for you is for an appointed time. I strongly believe the reason the Lord takes time to usher you into your destiny is that He has to prepare you for what He has prepared for you.

> But as it is written, Eye hath
> not seen, nor ear heard, neither
> have entered into the heart of
> man, the things which God hath
> prepared for them that love him.
> (1 Corinthians 2:9)

We can look at the example of David, who was a young shepherd boy before he became a great warrior. Being a shepherd boy, learning how to use the rod to pursue a lion and a bear, was a way of God preparing him to be bold enough to stand before the giant Goliath, using the same rod to strike down the giant, which eventually made him honorable in the eyes of the Israelites. They even sang a song for him, which displeased Saul, who became jealous of David and even tried to kill him (1 Samuel 18:7–9). No soldier prepares at the time of a battle but before the battle arises. In the same vein, the Lord takes time to prepare you before the manifestation of your great destiny because unpreparedness leads to frustration. That's why many people quit marriages, jobs, and businesses when they are not fully prepared for them. The blessing of God comes plain with no sorrow or pain attached, but it will be painful if you try to run ahead of God when it's not the right time for the fulfillment of the plan or destiny He has for you.

> This is what the Lord says: "*When seventy years are completed* [timing] for Babylon, I will come to you and *fulfill my good promise* [or plan] to bring you back to this place." (Jeremiah 29:10; italics added)

There is a lesson to learn from the life of Joseph. The Lord revealed His plan to him in a dream at the age of seventeen, letting him know that he was destined for greatness and that his brothers were going to bow down to him (Genesis 37:5–11). With such a great promise over the life of Joseph, it didn't exempt him from tests and trials. He was sold as a slave into a strange land and wrongfully put into prison, but the Lord lifted him to the throne in Egypt at the appointed time. When God has a plan or purpose for your life and when you don't run ahead of Him, trying to make it happen outside of His time, He will maneuver your way into the place of your destiny. Under no circumstance was Joseph going to leave Canaan by his own will to go into Egypt, where his destiny was. He testified that his brothers' hatred toward him by selling him into Egypt was meant for evil, but it was the vehicle used by the Lord to transport him into the land of his destiny to wait for his appointed time for God's promise to be fulfilled in his life (Genesis 41:40–41). The beauty of your life, marriage, business, career, and ministry is in God's time.

> Thou shalt arise and have mercy upon Zion: for the time to favor her, yea, *the set time*, has come. (Psalm 102:13; italics added)

> He hath made every thing beautiful in *His time*." (Ecclesiastes 3:11; italics added)

> To everything there is *a season*, and *a time* to every purpose under the heaven. (Ecclesiastes 3:1; italics added)

When you are in a hurry to fulfill destiny outside of God and His timing, you will suffer horror, lack, and frustration. Moses did not know that God destined him to be the deliverer for Israel at the age of eighty, but he tried to do it at forty. He suffered the consequence by running for his life in the desert. The Lord is not slack concerning His promises. You have to be committed to His timing to see His promises fulfilled in your life or ministry.

Another example you could learn from is Abraham. The Lord took him outside and told him to count the stars in the sky, making it known to him that as countless as the stars are, so will his descendants be while his wife, Sarai, was still barren. But there came an appointed time when the Lord visited Abraham to reassure him by giving him a specific time that his wife, Sarai, was going to conceive and give birth to the promised child, Isaac (Genesis 18).

> "Where is your wife Sarah?" they asked him. "There, in the tent," he said. Then one of them said, "*I will surely return to you about this time next year*, and Sarah your wife will have a son." (Genesis 18:9–10; italics added)

> Sarah became pregnant and bore a son to Abraham in his old age, *at the very time God had promised him.* (Genesis 21:2; italics added)

Every premature manifestation of a destiny or temporary success is an act of inappropriate timing of God's plan and purpose. God is interested in every aspect of our lives as believers. It wouldn't be lovely to an earthly father to choose just one part of a child's life. He will always want to be involved. There are certain things a father will not do or give to his children when the time is not right because they have not developed the capacity for what he wants to do or give them. You can't buy a car for a five-year-old child and give him the keys to drive; that will be the last time you see him. Or you can't take a toddler and put her in grade one instead of nursery. As preparation and development are necessary in the natural, so are things of the spirit. God will use every means to prepare and develop you for the great destiny He has for you, and when the fullness of time comes, He will exalt you. The full detail of your destiny is in the hands of God. You need to commit everything to Him to make it happen on His terms.

> Even so we, when we were children, were in bondage under the elements of the world: but *when the fulness of the time was come*, God sent forth his Son, made of a woman, made under the law, to redeem them that were under the law, that we might receive the adoption of sons. (Galatians 4:3–5; italics added)

Jesus was the Lamb slain before the foundation of the world, which means God had a plan of redemption before He created mankind. But He waited for the fullness of time to send our Lord Jesus Christ to fulfill His plan. He always follows that pattern concerning His plan and purpose for our lives. You don't need to panic. Your time is ever closer with God when He will turn everything around in your life, which will be like a dream of the night, and restore to you joy that will never leave your habitation.

> And Sarah said, *God hath made me to laugh* [at last], so that all that hear will laugh with me. And she said, Who would have said unto Abraham, that Sarah should have given children suck? For I have born him a son in his old age. (Genesis 21:6–7; italics added)

> When the LORD turned again the captivity of Zion, we were like them that dream. Then was our mouth *filled with laughter*, and our tongue with singing: then said they among the heathen, the LORD hath done great things for them. The LORD hath done great things for us; whereof we are glad. (Psalm 126:1–3; italics added)

Growing up as a less privileged child, things were very difficult for me. My parents had no good jobs. My mom had to wake up early, at 4:00–5:00 a.m., to buy palm nuts to sell before buying food late at night when she got home, which was sometimes our first meal for the day. Growing up with such a situation surrounding your life, you will be fully persuaded that's the conclusion of your destiny. Never climax your destiny based on the situation surrounding your life, and never limit your vision because of your current situation as a child of God. Your destiny, or future, is in the plan of God. My case seemed hopeless—not knowing where the next meal would come from when I was awake. Later in my life, I had no stable place to sleep because the land my father took care of for his cousin was later possessed by his children. As a teenager growing up in Liberia, I had many opportunities to be a bad child based on all the negative situations that surrounded my life. I strongly believe that the Holy Spirit laid it in my heart that the only way for every situation in my life to change was to draw closer to Jesus, and the Lord would include me in His plan for greatness.

When I fully committed myself to the Lord, took my eyes off the problem, and placed them on Jesus, He began to give me glimpses of my destiny. Let me say one thing to help you. There's no child of God—born again, walking in the light—to whom the Lord has not revealed His plan for their life.

"For I know the plans I have for you," declares the Lord, "plans to prosper you and not to harm you, plans to give you hope and a future." (Jeremiah 29:11)

However, as it is written: "What no eye has seen, what

no ear has heard, and what no human mind has conceived"—the things God has prepared for those who love him—*these are the things God has revealed to us by his Spirit.* The Spirit searches all things, even the deep things of God. (1 Corinthians 2:9–10; italics added)

The reason God does reveal His plan and purpose for our lives is so that we conduct ourselves by walking in the light to fulfill the destiny He has for us. Being revealed to me by the Spirit of the Lord that my beginning was not my ending filled my heart with joy through the trials.

I had a dream one night at the age of thirteen. I saw myself on a plane, and I landed in a strange nation with a different race but predominantly White. Waking up from such a dream and seeing yourself lying down in a small room, on a flat mattress without a bed board, with four other boys, you would get angry that you woke up in the first place at that age. Five years later, I had a similar dream again; and when the appointed time came at the age of twenty-one, a few days after my birthday, I landed in the United States of America. Since being in the US, the Lord has given me glimpses of the next phase of the destiny He has for me, but it is for an appointed time.

Jesus followed the pattern of divine timing when He was on this earth.

> His brethren therefore said unto him, Depart and go into Judea, that your disciples also may see the works that you do. Then Jesus said unto them, *My time is not yet come.* (John 7:3, 6; italics added)

When His time fully came to be glorified by the Father, the Lord has highly exalted Him forever.

> Wherefore God also hath highly exalted him, and given him a name which is above every name. (Philippians 2:9)

> These words spake Jesus, and lifted up his eyes to heaven, and said, Father, *the hour is come*; glorify thy Son, that thy Son also may glorify thee. (John 17:1; italics added)

Your time will come for the Lord to fulfill His plan and purpose for your life—the great ministry He has for you to fulfill, if you are called. Even though the beginning may seem small, stay faithful to the little group He has committed to you. If you are called, the great ministry He has for you will unfold. Also, if you are a layman, your life is not over until the Lord says so. The situation or circumstances shouldn't dictate your future. The Lord is still processing you for the great destiny He has prepared for you. As you walk with the Lord Jesus, He will continue to reveal your future to you by the Holy Spirit. I encourage you to write down the vision of your destiny. It shall surely speak at the appointed time.

# Chapter 2

# Divine Guidance

*And the LORD answered me, and said, Write
the vision, and make it plain upon tables, that
he may run that readeth it. For the vision is yet
for an appointed time, but at the end it shall
speak, and not lie: though it tarry, wait for it;
because it will surely come, it will not tarry.'*

—Habakkuk 2:2–3; reverse italics added

As every vision or destiny is for an appointed
time, divine direction is also necessary for it to be
actualized. The Lord didn't just give Habakkuk the
vision or His plan; He also instructed him on what
to do to see the vision come to pass. One consistent
trend of every great person in Scripture is that they
followed divine guidance. Divine guidance is a great
asset to every great destiny in the kingdom. The Lord
spoke to Abraham about what to do to step into the
greatness He wanted to make out of his life.

Now the Lord had said to
Abram: "Get out of your coun-

try, from your family And from your father's house, to a land that I will show you. I will make you a great nation…" So Abram departed as the Lord had spoken to him. (Genesis 12:1–2, 4)

You could have a full vision of your destiny; but the vision by itself, without direction, will be stagnant. If you are guided by the Lord in every area of your life, it will be more exciting because it is frustrating to wander around in the wilderness without knowing how to enter the promised land. Your promised land could be the marriage or business the Lord has ordained for you, or it could be ministry. It takes divine guidance to enjoy the full blessing of whatever the Lord has ordained for you. Seeking to lead yourself without seeking the direction of the Lord concerning any decision will make life difficult for you. God is interested in every little detail about your life. Never leave Him out of the equation. He's the one that holds your future. Even though your destiny is in His hands, He will not impose His will on you if you seek to walk in your own ways instead of following His direction. He is only committed to guiding you if you will commit to following Him.

I will instruct thee and teach thee in the way which thou shalt go I will guide thee with mine eye. (Psalm 32:8)

> The steps of a good man
> are ordered by the LORD: and
> he delighteth in his way. (Psalm
> 37:23)

Kenneth E. Hagin gave a testimony of a successful businessman who was in one of the churches he pastored. He asked him about the secret of his success in business. The man told him that whenever someone came to him with a business deal or investment that seemed good by his physical senses, he always took time to seek God, sometimes in a three-day fast and prayer, to hear what the Lord would drop in his spirit before making any investment. When he had the green light in his spirit, he went ahead to invest; and if there was a red flag, he wouldn't. Over the years, this member of his church experienced a financial increase in millions.

> Trust in the LORD with all
> thine heart; and lean not unto
> thine own understanding. In all
> thy ways acknowledge him, and
> He shall direct thy paths. (Proverbs 3:5–6)

Bishop David Oyedepo gives a testimony about the success of our ministry, Winner's Chapel, which is making a global impact. Where the headquarters is situated today was at the direction of the Lord. According to him, he had planned to take the church to a location without the direction of the Lord. By the mercy of the Lord, He guided him to the city where the church is now seating fifty thousand members, and a one-hundred-thousand-seat construction is going on to accommodate the crowd. When the Lord led him to the location of the church, he couldn't accept it by his physical senses because the entire place was a forest, and it was far from the rest of the city. It was popular for everyone to have their church in the city for their members to have easy access. But after viewing the forest and praising the Lord, he heard the voice of the Lord saying, "This is the place." Today, the forest is a city by the direction of the Lord. The Lord later told Bishop David Oyedepo that if he had taken the ministry where he planned without His direction, it would have been the end of the ministry.

Let me point out something to help you. The blessing of God is not limited to a geographical location. It is tied to divine direction. If God is the one guiding you, His blessings will accompany you. There was a famine in the land of Canaan, where Isaac was dwelling. He wanted to go down to Egypt, as it was a city of prosperity and opportunity in those days. I believe everyone was leaving Canaan to travel to Egypt because of the famine. Isaac wanted to leave for Egypt, but the Lord told him not to leave because Canaan was his place of destiny.

> And the LORD appeared
> unto him, and said, Go not down
> into Egypt; dwell in the land

which I shall tell thee of: sojourn in this land, and I will be with thee, and will bless thee. (Genesis 26:2–3)

Then Isaac sowed in that land, and received in the same year [of famine] an hundredfold: and the LORD blessed him. And the man waxed great, and went forward, and grew until he became very great. (Genesis 26:12–13)

There are many who have missed out on their destiny because of wrong decisions made without seeking God's direction. We live in a world today where everyone is patterning their lives after another, following the path of others without seeking the path of the Lord. One of the secrets to David's success was following divine guidance. No wonder every battle he fought at the direction of the Lord, he won. Following divine direction guarantees you a life of consistent victory.

And David enquired at the LORD, saying, Shall I pursue after this troop? Shall I overtake them? And he answered him, Pursue: for thou shalt surely overtake them, and without fail recover all. (1 Samuel 30:8)

Never pursue when the Lord has not told you to pursue. Always inquire of Him before taking any step or embarking on any plan. Whenever you move ahead of God without seeking His guidance, you will come against many obstacles and face difficulties. But when you seek His guidance, it will save you from trouble and difficulties. There is a destiny (e.g., marriage, business, career, or ministry) God destined for you; it takes seeking His guidance to fulfill it.

I am a victim of many wrong decisions that cost me money and wasted effort and almost cost me my life. This may sound scary to you, but it's true. Pastor or layman, not walking in the will of the Lord could cost you your life. If you are not on God's territory, you are trespassing on the devil's territory, which gives him all the right to tie down everything in your life and, sadly, destroy your life. It is very essential to seek the Lord to show you which path to take in life.

As a young man in Liberia, when I commit to attending church services seated on the front row, something always told me that I belonged behind the pulpit. Not being sensitive to the leading of God by the Spirit, I ignored it. I remember that when I grew up spiritually, I realized it was the Lord trying to direct my steps concerning my destiny.

When I came to the US, being passionate about becoming a politician, I applied for admission to obtain a degree in government, politics, and policy. Throughout my study at the university, I wasn't happy. I believed something was wrong. One lesson I want you to learn is that you will never find happiness outside of God's will for your life and ignoring His guidance. You could have temporary joy, but it won't exempt you from depression. When you are in God's will for your life and following His guidance, it makes your journey in life exciting and fills your life with joy and peace that surpasses all understanding.

My decision to choose a career path without inquiring of the Lord explains why many believers obtain two to three degrees, including PhDs, and still suffer stagnation. It will save you a lot of energy from wasted effort by acknowledging the Lord in everything for Him to direct your path to your destiny.

When I obtained my degree, I went to the Lord, asking Him to show me how to go about my political career. I prayed throughout the day and thanked Him for the journey. I had a vision the next day. In this vision, I was above the roof of my apartment with two men. Above us, in the clouds, was Jesus standing on a white cloud with the globe in His right hand. In this vision, these two guys were in a debate about the existence of God. Hearing their conversation, I went to them to give them clarity about God, and I said to them, "If you see who I'm seeing, you won't argue that there isn't a God, but I'm seeing Jesus above us." Right away, the vision disappeared. While wondering about the meaning of the vision, the Lord brought to my memory how the apostle Paul was in defense of the gospel. I began to question myself: *Is the Lord calling me to preach?*

A week later, I had a dream. In this dream, I saw myself at a crusade in Africa. I preached until one of the pastors told me it was time for the people to go home. When I woke up from that dream, I knew right away the Lord's plan for me was to preach, not to be a politician. What I should have done earlier—seeking the Lord for direction before embarking on a career path—I did later. It could have saved me money and time pursuing a degree without God's direction. The reason you need to seek God's guidance before making any decision is that He knows the future and how to get you there.

> As a bird that wandered from her nest, so is a man that wandered from his place [of destiny if he doesn't seek God's guidance]. (Proverbs 27:8)

> The Lord will guide you always; *he will satisfy your needs in a sun-scorched land* and will strengthen your frame. You will be like a well-watered garden, like a spring whose waters never fail. (Isaiah 58:11; italics added)

> *They did not thirst when he led them* through the deserts; he made water flow for them from the rock; he split the rock and water gushed out. (Isaiah 48:21; italics added)

When you follow the guidance of the Lord, He destroys every obstacle in your path for you to arrive safely at your glorious destiny or future. Your great destiny, marriage, business, career, or ministry rest on you following God's guidance. There is nothing the Lord wants you to do that He's not willing to help you do. There is nowhere in life the Lord wants you to go that He's not willing to help you reach. There is nothing the Lord wants you to obtain that He won't help you obtain, but it's at His discretion and following His direction that commits His involvement in your affairs. That's the secret David learned by saying, "The Lord is my shepherd, I shall not want or lack [e.g., strength, guidance, resources, finances]." The job of the shepherd is to protect and guide his flock in and out of the fold. Jesus is the Good Shepherd. He is fully committed to guiding your life on the right path to fulfill your destiny.

Write the vision as it is revealed to you by the Lord concerning your destiny, ministry, career, marriage, or business. As it is for an appointed time, seek the Lord, who has the full details of your future or destiny, and ask Him to guide you on how to see it fulfilled in your life as you wait for God to make it happen in His time.

# Chapter 3

# Power of Patience

*For the vision is yet for an appointed time,*
*but at the end it shall speak, and not*
*lie:* though it tarry, wait for it; *because*
*it will surely come, it will not tarry.*

—Habakkuk 2:3; reverse italics added

Every aspect concerning vision is essential. If one is missing or not followed, a vision or destiny will be destroyed. A vision or great destiny is for an appointed time and requires divine guidance. Patience is one of the keys to its fulfillment. The Lord told Habakkuk to tarry or wait long enough. Even though His plan will take longer, it will surely come to pass if you do not faint. We live in a world today where patience is disregarded. Everyone is in a hurry to fulfill destiny, following worldly patterns instead of godly patterns, which require time, divine direction, patience, etc. When God reveals His plan and purpose for your life or ministry, that doesn't mean it will happen tomorrow. As you receive the vision, write it down and make it plain, then continue to revisit the vision by reading it to remind yourself of God's plan and purpose for your life. Also, wait patiently for God to bring it to pass.

Many great destinies have been destroyed because of impatience. We see that with the entire generation that perished in the wilderness. Every time things didn't go the way they expected, they murmured and wanted to go back to Egypt, saying their situation in Egypt was much better than their situation in the wilderness. Their impatience from the onset of their journey from Egypt through the wilderness contributed to their unbelief and doubt, which caused them to miss out on the Promised Land.

> For we dare not make ourselves of the number, or compare ourselves with some that commend themselves: but they measuring themselves by themselves, and comparing themselves among themselves, are not wise.
> (2 Corinthians 10:12)

Patience is one of the fruits imparted into your spirit by the Holy Spirit as a child of God. He expects you to exercise patience toward His plan or promises over your life or ministry. In the process of waiting or being patient concerning the great destiny God has for you, you gain a clearer understanding of what the Lord wants to accomplish in your life. It is by waiting or patience that direction comes from the Lord about a vision or destiny. It is through patience that God reveals to you who to marry if you are not in a hurry outside of God's timing. Patience imparts unto you divine ideas that will help your destiny. Patience helps you renew your strength, increases anointing, and helps you gain more ground speed to usher you into a new height in life or ministry. Every great destiny, ministry, marriage, business, and career thrives by divine timing, guidance, and patience.

> They that *wait upon the* LORD shall renew their strength; *they shall mount up with wings as eagles* [soar high in life, not at the bottom]; they shall run, and not be weary; and they shall walk, and not faint.[Many are worried and depressed because of impatience.] (Isaiah 40:31; italics added)

> Wait on the LORD: Be of good courage, and he shall strengthen thine heart: *wait, I say, on the* LORD. (Psalm 27:14; italics added)

Not to mention names, but a testimony of a great man of God who is doing great in ministry almost missed out on the great ministry he's running today because of impatience. From the beginning of his ministry, the Lord trusted him with thirty members in his church as preparation for the thirty thousand members He had for him. As a result of the small growth of the ministry, he began to question the call of God on his life. He decided to go into full-time business instead of full-time ministry. He got tied up with making money instead of helping the flocks of God. His membership declined, and he eventually quit pastoring.

During a revival meeting, a word of knowledge was given by the pastor who was preaching that was related to this minister.

"Remember, My word says the gifts and calling of God are without repentance. I called you and placed a level of My anointing upon you to feed My flocks, but you were unfaithful due to greed and impatience. If you were unfaithful with the thirty flocks, how can I trust you with the thirty thousand flocks? I, who commanded the locusts to flow into Egypt and called the frogs from every river and swamp to cover the land, don't you think I'm able to draw multitudes to Myself if you are faithful and patient? My call is still upon you. It's left to what you do with the call that will release My blessing in your life and ministry."

When this minister heard this, he knew that was the Lord speaking to him through this pastor. He got back into the ministry, began from scratch, and remained patient, and today he's running a large ministry with more than thirty thousand members with a few network churches around the globe. The great destiny the Lord has for you requires you to endure patiently to obtain the promise. Do not backslide from

God's divine will for your life because things are not turning out the way you want. Just remain faithful and patient in that ministry, marriage, business, or career if He's the one directing you, and He will bless it.

> For when God made promise to Abraham, because he could swear by no greater, he swore by himself, saying, Surely blessing I will bless you, and multiplying I will multiply you. *And so, after he had patiently endured* he obtained the promise. (Hebrews 6:13–15; italics added)

If you are not willing to endure patiently, there is no greatness that will manifest in your life. Before you can reach the peak of your destiny, there are mountains to climb and rivers to cross, but never allow the height of the mountain or the wave of the river to scare you away from your destiny. No matter the circumstances that surround you, don't give up because the blessing and promises of God require patience.

> Behold, we count them happy which endure. Ye have heard of the patience of Job, and have seen the end of the Lord; that the Lord is very pitiful, and of tender mercy. (James 5:11)

Rest in the LORD, and wait patiently for him: fret not thyself because of him who prospereth in his way, because of the man who bringeth wicked devices to pass. (Psalm 37:7)

For ye have need of patience, that, after ye have done the will of God, ye might receive the promise. (Hebrews 10:36)

If the Word of God says you need patience, that means it is a necessity for every greatness in the kingdom. Job, through his affliction, remained patient with the Lord. He did not cast away his confidence concerning the promise and almightiness of God. The Lord blessed the latter end of Job more than his beginning and restored to him twice all his losses.

And the LORD turned the captivity of Job, when he prayed for his friends: also the LORD gave Job twice as much as he had before." (Job 42:10)

All the days of my appointed time will I wait, till my change come. (Job 14:14)

# Test of Patience

There is no breakthrough without breakdowns. There will be periods of tests and trials. Being a child of God and having a promise of greatness over your life does not exempt you from tests. In fact, the Word of God says, "Many are the afflictions of the righteous, but the LORD delivers him out of them all" (Psalm 37:29).

Every great man you admire in Scripture has stories behind their greatness. Elisha, before God told Elijah to cast his mantle upon him to be a prophet in his place, was a farmer. Before David received the anointing as king, priest, and prophet, he was a shepherd boy. Joseph, before he became a prime minister, was in prison. He waited patiently until the day came for God to change his destiny. Father Abraham was told by the Lord that he was going to be great and multiply his seed. That didn't happen the next day or the following year. He endured patiently before the Lord brought His promise to pass and changed his destiny. Forever the name of Abraham will not be erased from the earth, but it came at the expense of his obedience and patience. The same principle applies to the greatness the Lord wants to bring out of your life or ministry. Whatever God's plan is for you, He will bring it to pass. You need to be patient for the appointed time to see it fulfilled.

> God is not human, that he
> should lie, not a human being,

that he should change his mind.
Does he speak and then not act?
Does he promise and not fulfill?
(Numbers 23:19 NIV)

Keep in mind that the LORD
your God is [the only] God. He
is a faithful God, who keeps his
promise and is merciful to thou-
sands of generations of those who
love him and obey his commands.
(Deuteronomy 7:9 GWT)

No matter the trials or circumstances that are against you, remain patient and consecrated to the plan and purpose of God. Joseph didn't become a ruler in Egypt at seventeen when the Lord revealed to him his vision or destiny. The Lord made him great at the age of thirty after he went through the trials of betrayal by his brothers and false accusations by his master's wife. Neither the devil nor his agent can stop the plan and purpose of God for your life if you remain patient for the appointed time for the fulfillment of your great destiny.

Write the vision concerning your destiny, ministry, business, career, etc. and make it plain on tablets, "for the vision is yet for an appointed time; but at the end it will speak, and it will not lie. Though it tarries, be patient because it will surely come; it will not tarry" (Habakkuk 2:2–3 NKJV).

# Chapter 4

# The Act of Faith

*For the vision is yet for an appointed time,
but at the end it shall speak, and not
lie: though it tarry, wait for it; because
it will surely come, it will not tarry.*

—Habakkuk 2:3

*As it is written, I have made thee a father of
many nations, before him whom* he believed…
*who against hope* believed in hope, *that he
might become the father of many nations,
according to that* which was spoken, *So shall
thy seed be.* And being not weak in faith, *he
considered not his own body now dead, when
he was about an hundred years old, neither yet
the deadness of Sarah's womb:* he staggered
not at the promise of God through unbelief;
but was strong in faith, *giving glory to God;
and* being fully persuaded *that, what he
had promised, he was able also to perform.*

—Romans 4:17–21; reverse italics added

One can be patient long enough in unbelief and doubt, having no expectation. Faith is the expectation of things hoped for. While you wait patiently for the vision or plan and purpose of God to come to pass in your life, you must add faith to patience. All the promises are obtainable by faith. Abraham was patient when God promised that He was going to make him great and had already made him a father of many nations while it was yet to be seen. He was not in unbelief or doubt but was strong in faith, being fully persuaded that the Lord would be able to fulfill His promise. You won't enter into the great destiny God has for you without being fully persuaded by the almightiness of God that He's able to fulfill His plan and purpose in your life.

The children of Israel missed out on the Promised Land because of fear. They were not convinced or persuaded by the almightiness of God when they spied the land that the Lord, who sent them to view the land, was able to deal with their enemies that dwelled in the land.

> We went into the land to which you sent us, and it does flow with milk and honey! Here is its fruit. *But the people who live there are powerful,* and the cities are fortified and very large. We even saw descendants of Anak there. (Numbers 13:2, 27–28; italics added)

> And there we saw the giants, the sons of Anak, which come of the giants: and we were in our own sight as grasshoppers, and so we were in their sight. (Numbers 13:32–33)

> And he said unto them, Why are ye so fearful? how is it that ye have no faith? (Mark 4:40)

The number one enemy of victory is fear. When the Philistine giant defied the entire army of Israel and no one could go against him, it was because of fear. If they had taken their eyes off themselves or their limitations and trusted in God, I strongly believe it wouldn't have been long before God delivered Goliath into their hands. There was a little shepherd boy named David who refused to be a slave to fear and trusted in God, and he was victorious over Goliath. From that day onward, the Lord began to work with David and made him one of the greatest people who ever walked this planet. You need to cooperate with God through your faith to bring to reality His plan and purpose for your life and ministry.

> David said moreover, The LORD that delivered me out of the paw of the lion, and out of the paw of the bear, he will deliver

> me out of the hand of this Philistine. And Saul said unto David, Go, and the LORD be with thee. (1 Samuel 17:37)

> Through faith they subdued kingdoms, wrought righteousness, *obtained promises*, stopped the mouths of lions. (Hebrews 11:33; italics added)

The heroes of faith obtained promises from God. I believe their greatness rested on their strong faith in God, which caused Him to fulfill His promises in their lives. They subdued kingdoms, ran through a troop, and took possession of what their enemies took from them. The enemy will endeavor to stop the plan and purpose of God from being fulfilled in your life. It is by the force of faith that you dispossess him of all that is yours. Faith is one of the tenets upon which all that we receive from God is based. This implies that you won't get what you want from God if you don't develop and exercise faith in Him. If you live or walk by your physical senses instead of faith, you will be defeated every time because your physical senses will make every problem seem impossible. But by faith in God, all things are possible.

> For we walk by faith, not by sight [our physical senses]. (2 Corinthians 5:7)

> But without *faith* it is impos-
> sible to please God. (Hebrews
> 11:6; italics added)

What pleases God is having full confidence in Him that He is able to deliver on His promises. That was the secret of Abraham's success. You know it takes faith to sojourn into a strange land, leaving all that you are familiar with, but he departed based on the Lord's instruction. The Bible says Abraham departed without doubt because he believed God (Genesis 12). Faith will keep you above the challenges of life. Having a clearer understanding of what faith is will help you get rid of your doubt and fear and be fully persuaded that God will bring to pass His plan and purpose for your life.

## What is faith?

Faith is total dependency and confidence in God and His Word. David said to Goliath, "This day the Lord will deliver you into my hand, and I will strike you and take your head from you. And this day I will give the carcasses of the Philistines to the birds of the air and the wild beasts of the earth, that all the earth may know that there is a God in Israel" (1 Samuel 17:46). Goliath felt insulted by the little boy's bold declaration. God is not a respecter of persons or age, but He has great respect for and honors faith. Faith is the gateway to unlimited possibilities.

> Jesus said…, If thou canst believe, all things are possible to him that believeth. (Mark 9:23)

> Now faith is being sure [without doubt] of what we hope for [e.g., finances, healing, or marriage], being convinced of what we do not seen. (Hebrews 11:1)

If you wait to see the manifestation of those things you hope for before believing, you won't have them. You have to be convinced by faith that you have them when they are unseen, and it will become a reality. Faith is full persuasion of God's Word by ignoring the unwanted circumstances and believing the Word (Romans 4:17–21). The Word of God will not work for you unless you are fully persuaded it is so. The promises of God from His Word won't become a reality in your life until you believe that He is able to perform or bring to pass that which is spoken from His word.

> The Lord said to me, "You have seen correctly, for I am watching to see that my word is fulfilled." (Jeremiah 1:12)

Faith is the difference maker in every sphere of life. It never returns defeated. You are redeemed for signs and wonders, but signs and wonders won't accompany you without faith, which invokes the mighty hand of God to change your destiny. Faith is a spiritual weapon used to defeat the devil in every combat.

> Above all, taking the shield
> of faith, wherewith ye shall be
> able to quench all the fiery darts
> of the wicked. (Ephesians 6:16)

Paul described faith as a shield because, when a nation went against another, a shield was used to block the artillery fired against every individual. It quenched the effect of the arrows fired against an army or an individual. The days we are living in are evil. There are arrows of financial hardship, sickness, disease, and untimely death being fired into the atmosphere. To quench the effects of these arrows, you must make faith your shield daily, which will always cause you to triumph. Faith despises every negative report (e.g., doctor's report—sickness, poverty, barrenness) and believes the report of God, which is His written Word.

> For by faith the elders
> obtained a good report. (Hebrews
> 11:2)

By faith, the three Hebrew boys—Shadrach, Meshach, and Abednego—dared King Nebuchadnezzar not to worship his god, and by faith, they believed God was able to deliver them from the blazing furnace (Daniel 3:17). By faith, Daniel defied King Darius, continuing to pray to his God instead of the god of Babylon. By faith, he trusted in God to deliver him from the lion's den (Daniel 6:16–22). By faith, Joshua commanded the sun to stand still and the moon to stop in the sky until the Amorites, who were skilled in night battle, were defeated (Joshua 10:12–13).

These definitions of faith and examples give you a better understanding of the importance of faith in the actualization of destiny in the kingdom. The Lord tested the obedience and faith of Abraham by telling him to offer his only son, Isaac, for whom he had waited many years and whom he had believed God for. Being obedient and a man of faith, he rose up early in the morning without hesitation and took his son to offer him as a burnt offering to the Lord.

Here is where I want to draw your attention.

> Isaac spoke up and said to his father Abraham, "Father?"
>
> "Yes, my son?" Abraham replied.
>
> "The fire and wood are here," Isaac said, "but where is the lamb for the burnt offering?"
>
> Abraham answered, "*God himself will provide the lamb for*

*the burnt offering*, my son." (Genesis 22:7–8; italics added).

Abraham had full confidence that God would provide a lamb for the burnt offering. Even if he had to kill Isaac, he believed the Lord was able to replace him. Based on his believing and saying, the Lord did provide a lamb and swore a blessing upon him because He was pleased with his faith. Without faith, God will not be pleased with you to bring to pass His plan and purpose for your life.

## Bold Declaration

Remember, Abraham didn't just believe in what God was going to do. He declared boldly, "God himself will provide the lamb for the burnt offering, my son." It was in declaring boldly what he believed that moved God to provide for Himself a lamb. His declaration caught the attention of God, changing his destiny and making him great.

> I am the Lord your God, who brought you up out of Egypt. Open wide your mouth, and I will fill it [with good things]. (Psalm 81:10)

To have faith is important, but just believing won't produce any results. To achieve what you believe, you must speak it. The authority of your faith is expressed by speaking boldly what you believe. When you are timid to speak what you believe, it is because you are doubtful, and that is referred to as little faith. Great or strong faith is believing and speaking without fear.

> It is written: "I believed; therefore I have spoken." Since we have that same spirit of faith, we also believe and therefore speak. (2 Corinthians 4:13)

> And Jesus answering saith unto them, Have faith in God. For verily I say unto you, that whosoever *shall say* unto this mountain, be thou removed, and be thou cast into the sea; and shall not doubt in his heart, but *shall believe* that those things which *he saith* shall come to pass; *he shall have whatsoever he saith.* (Mark 11:22–23; italics added)

Jesus makes it clear that believing and saying will move the mountain. A mountain could be an impossible situation in your life. It could be sickness, disease, financial hardship, etc. Believe that with God, all things are possible, and that when you speak to the problem, it will obey. Your word is the game changer in every situation. Jesus spoke to the wind, and it obeyed. He commanded sicknesses and evil spirits out of many with a word. He cursed the fig tree to die with a word. You know by faith and a spoken word from God, the world was framed or created (Hebrews 11:3). You find in Genesis 1 a lot of "And God said" because saying what you desire to see as you believe is what produces results in your life. Whatever God wanted to see at creation, He spoke, and they were created (Psalm 33:9).

> And God said, Let there be light: and there was light. (Genesis 1:3)

> And God said, Let there be a firmament in the midst of the waters, and let it divide the waters from the waters. Genesis 1:6)

> And God said, Let the waters under the heaven be gathered together unto one place, and let the dry land appear: and it was so. (Genesis 1:9)

> And God said, Let the earth bring forth grass, the herb yielding seed, and the fruit tree yielding fruit after his kind, whose seed is in itself, upon the earth: and it was so. (Genesis 1:11)

And God said, Let there be lights in the firmament of the heaven to divide the day from the night; and let them be for signs, and for seasons, and for days, and years. (Genesis 1:14)

And God said, Let the waters bring forth abundantly the moving creature that hath life, and fowl that may fly above the earth in the open firmament of heaven. (Genesis 1:20)

And God said, Let the earth bring forth the living creature after his kind, cattle, and creeping thing, and beast of the earth after his kind: and it was so. (Genesis 1:24)

To see in your life what you believe, you must say it, for you shall have whatsoever you say. We see how the Lord hearkened to the spoken word of Joshua and caused nature to obey him when the army of Israel was not skilled in fighting at night as their enemies were trained.

On the day the Lord gave the Amorites over to Israel, *Joshua said* to the Lord in the presence of Israel: *"Sun, stand still over Gibeon, and you, moon, over the Valley of Aijalon." So the sun stood still, and the moon stopped* [as he spoke] *till the nation avenged itself on its enemies.* (Joshua 10:12–13; italics added)

The Lord is not a respecter of persons. He is a respecter of the principles of faith, which always please Him. He is more pleased to deliver on His promise not by you just believing but by also speaking, which is proof of your full confidence in the integrity of His Word. Hold fast to the confession of your faith without wavering (Hebrews 10:23). Do not change your confession no matter how huge your physical sense may make it seem. For faith to work for you positively, your saying should always be consistent with what you believe. I used the word *positively* because your faith can work for you negatively when you make the wrong confession.

Your words are a seed of your faith. When it is sown, it produces fruit. As Bro. Hagin once said, "When you speak, it's your faith speaking whether positive or negative." You will never reap anything in your life that is contrary to what you believe and speak. With the heart, we believe first; and with the mouth, we make a confession of what we believe. So when you speak, you are expressing your faith, which will produce fruit.

# THE ACT OF FAITH

Let me draw your attention to few scriptures about the importance of words.

> Thou shalt also decree a thing, and it shall be established unto thee: and the light shall shine upon thy ways. (Job 22:28)

If your path is full of light and good things or full of darkness and rough, it's the result of your declarations or what you have been saying.

> He shall have whatsoever he saith. (Mark 11:23)

> Words from the mouth of the wise are gracious, but fools are consumed by their own lips. (Ecclesiastes 10:12)

> Those who guard their lips preserve their lives, but those who speak rashly will come to ruin. (Proverbs 13:3)

You can ruin everything God has for you and will not enjoy the full blessing of God by negative confessions of faith.

> Out of the same mouth proceedeth blessing and cursing.

> My brethren, these things ought
> not so to be. (James 3:10)

When you believe and speak positively, God intervenes to bring into existence what you say for your benefit. On the contrary, when you speak negatively, Satan intervenes to bring into existence what you say against yourself.

> You have been trapped by
> what you said, ensnared by the
> words of your mouth. (Proverbs
> 6:2)

> Say unto them, As truly as
> I live, saith the LORD, as ye have
> spoken in mine ears, so will I do
> to you. (Numbers 14:28)

Did you notice what the Lord says? He said, "As you have spoken," which means God will do nothing contrary to what you have spoken. Negative words will hinder you from obtaining the promises of God, as the children of Israel didn't enter the Promised Land except Caleb and Joshua, who didn't look at the giants (circumstances) in the land but believed God and spoke the right words.

> Then Caleb silenced the peo-
> ple before Moses and said, *"We*
> *should go up and take possession of*

*the land, for we can certainly do it."* But the men who had gone up with him said, "We can't attack those people; they are stronger than we are." And they spread among the Israelites a bad report about the land they had explored. They said, "The land we explored devours those living in it. All the people we saw there are of great size." (Numbers 13:30–32; italics added)

There is no situation in your life that is greater than God. He is the almighty, all-sufficient God. You are a promised child moving about with a great destiny. The Lord may have spoken or revealed to you your future or His plan and purpose for your comfort. Write the vision; it's for an appointed time, but it will take faith to move the hand of God to fulfill it.

# Chapter 5

# The Power of Prayer

Prayer is the midwife that brings forth prophecy and great destiny. It is on the platform of prayer that humanity cooperates with God for His will to be done on the earth. When you are pregnant with a great destiny and waiting for the appointed time for delivery, you must travail in prayer.

> Who hath heard such a thing? Who hath seen such things? Shall the earth be made to bring forth in one day? Or shall a nation be born at once? For as soon as Zion travailed, she brought forth her children. (Isaiah 66:8)

The devil will endeavor to abort the great destiny the Lord has for you because he is on an assignment to steal, kill, and destroy. Prayer is a spiritual investment for a great future. When you invest physically in the natural, you don't benefit from it the next day; it takes time before you begin to see the return on your investment. So it is with prayer. There are prayers you pray now whose answers are not seen immediately, but they will surely pave the way for your destiny. It is good to be patient and wait for God and the appointed time for the vision or destiny of your ministry, business, marriage, or career. However, the devil will try to attack anything that will set you above, not beneath. It is prayer that aborts all the agendas of the devil and allows you to see the actualization of the great destiny the Lord has for you.

> And he spake a parable unto
> them to this end, that men ought
> always to pray, and not to faint.
> (Luke 18:1)

You are a child of destiny. As a child of God, you are redeemed as kings and priests on the earth. Jesus obtained for you a life of royalty. The devil will try to sit on the great destiny, ministry, marriage, business, or career God has for you. You have to resist him on the platform of prayer to disrupt all of his agenda against your life and destiny.

> Is any among you afflicted
> [going through trials]? Let him
> pray. (James 5:13)

Prayer is the solution to all of life's situations. It is vital to greatness. Prayer is the initiator of God's intervention in human affairs. Most often, many believe that God will automatically intervene in every situation or their affairs. If that were the case, Jesus wouldn't have told us to ask, and it shall be given. He would have said, "Wait, and it shall be given. Stand, and you will see it happen. Sleep, and the situation will disappear." Instead, He said, "Ask, and it will be given to you; seek, and you will find; knock, and it will be opened to you. For everyone who asks receives, and he who seeks finds, and to him who knocks it will be opened" (Matthew 7:7–8). Many have watched their destiny fold and conclude by the devil because of their laziness in praying until the plan of God for their lives comes to pass. It is true God has a great future for you; you have to force His will to be done in your life by diligently seeking Him through prayer. He will reward you and make your life great.

Everything in the kingdom of God does not come automatically. It is based on man's cooperation with God. One way in which we cooperate with God to have Him intervene in our affairs is through prayer. When there was a famine in Samaria because of the drought, the Lord promised there was going to be rain. If you notice in 1 Kings 18:1–2, 41–42, rain didn't come automatically when the Lord promised it. Elijah cooperated with God by climbing to the top of Mount Carmel, bowing low to the ground, and praying earnestly until it rained, and the problems they had growing their crops and raising their livestock ceased.

John Wesley, the founder of the Methodist church, once said, "God does nothing but in response to prayer." He meant believers' prayer because the prayer of the saints (the righteous) avails much. I believe the testimony of Kenneth E. Hagin about his wife will help you understand the point made by John Wesley. Brother Hagin's wife had a goiter, and it was growing larger, causing her to have choking spells. The doctor told her that she had to have surgery. He went to God in prayer about the situation. Each time he prayed about it, he always knew that if his wife went for the surgery, she was going to die. So he had that fear of letting her go for the surgery. He continued praying for his wife's health.

One day, Jesus appeared to him in a vision. The Lord said, "Tell your wife to go for the surgery. She will not die. It was divinely ordained that she was going to die during the surgery, but because you asked Me, she will live and not die. How I wish to do so much for My children only if they will ask Me." Even afterward, his wife knew in her spirit that she was going to die if she went for the surgery. What changed the situation? What got the Lord's attention to intervene in the situation? It was consistent prayer that moved the Lord Jesus to deliver his wife from death and extend her lifespan. The Lord did that in response to prayer. We see a similar situation with Hezekiah when he was appointed to die, but the Lord responded to his prayer and changed the situation.

In those days was Hezekiah
sick unto death. And Isaiah the

prophet the son of Amoz came unto him, and said unto him, Thus saith the LORD, Set thine house in order: for thou shalt die, and not live. Then Hezekiah turned his face toward the wall, and *prayed unto the Lord,* then came the word of the LORD to Isaiah, saying, Go, and say to Hezekiah, Thus saith the, the God of David thy father, *I have heard thy prayer,* I have seen thy tears: behold, *I will add unto thy days fifteen years.* (Isaiah 38:1–2, 4–5)

Divine cooperation with God through prayer is the enforcer of the actualization of vision or destiny. It takes prayer to bring God down to deal with every opposition against your destiny and set you over all circumstances. When the devil senses that you have a great destiny, you become attractive to him. Every great destiny attracts demonic opposition. No criminal will attempt a robbery at your house if he hasn't sensed anything of value. The devil will not waste his energy on you if he hasn't sensed greatness hovering over your life. He will fight for greatness not to settle in your life. Prayer invokes the mighty hands of God to settle your life and destiny.

It was prayer that moved the hand of God to deliver Peter supernaturally from prison by an angel while he awaited death the next day (Acts 12:5–7).

> For a great door and effectual is opened unto me, and there are many adversaries. (1 Corinthians 16:9)

## Its importance

Knowing the importance of prayer will help you understand why prayer is a vital key to the fulfillment of destiny. Prayer is a weapon that disrupts the agendas of the devil against your life and destiny. It will build a wall of fire around your life, protecting you from the attacks of the devil. The Lord has a great plan and purpose for your life, but you enforce His will and agenda for your life through prayer. It will break any limit the devil places on your life, ministry, business, marriage, or career. Prayer is an invitation that grants God permission to deal with every problem in your life.

When Hannah was mocked for being barren, she prayed; and God intervened, granting her a child named Samuel, who became a prophet in Israel (1 Samuel 1:6–11). Jabez cried out to the God of Israel, saying, "Oh, that you would bless me and enlarge my territory! Let your hand be with me and keep me from harm so that I will be free from pain." And God granted his request (1 Chronicles 4:10). Jabez prayed for enlargement, a change of destiny. His mother named him Jabez, which means sorrow, based on her pain. He refused to live under the bondage of that name. He sought the Lord for enlargement or greatness, and the Lord granted his request. Greatness was already hovering over his life; it only needed to be hatched, and prayer did that for him.

Prayer will divert the demonic wind blowing over your life or ministry that is driving away your congregation or preventing good things from reaching your hands. I invited an individual who was doing well in every aspect of life to join our prayer group. He told me that he didn't need prayer. Ignorantly, he said there was nothing to pray about because everything was going well. What he didn't understand was that at every height the Lord takes you, there is a greater height. He was proud and comfortable where he was. He failed to realize that with every rise in life, Satan assigns a higher demon to escort your journey. When I last saw this individual, everything had fallen apart. He was in debt financially, and one of his sons had run away from home and was heavily on drugs.

Prayer is one of the greatest defenses against all the weapons of the devil. As great as David was, he prayed for an increase and another dimension of greatness. Not only that, but he prayed for comfort on every side. That tells you that as great as you become, the devil will loose all his weapon against you to crash your destiny. When you rest on the wings of prayer, you fly above all the devices of the enemy.

> Thou shalt increase my greatness, and comfort me on every side. (Psalm 71:21)

It is through prayer that the will of God is known, and guidance is given by the spirit of God.

> As they ministered to the Lord, and *fasted [and prayed], the Holy Ghost said,* Separate me Barnabas and Saul for the work whereunto I have called them. And when they had fasted and prayed, and laid their hands on them, they sent them away. (Acts 13:2–3)

> "For I know the plans I have for you," declares the Lord, "plans to prosper you and not to harm you, plans to give you hope and a future. Then you will call on me and come and pray to me, and I will listen to you." (Jeremiah 29:11–12)

Prayer strengthens your spirit and keeps you in constant fellowship with God. The disciples were in constant fellowship with God through prayer in the Upper Room while they awaited the promise of the Spirit. While you await the great plan and purpose of

God for your life or ministry, continue to tune your spirit to heaven through constant prayer to obtain guidance and enforce the will of God for your life. Pray without ceasing until what God has promised or the great destiny that is hovering over your life is seen in your life or ministry.

# Chapter 6

# Blessedness of Consecration

*Wherefore come out from among them, and be ye separate, saith the Lord, and touch not the unclean thing; and I will receive you, and will be a father unto you, and ye shall be my sons and daughters, saith the Lord Almighty.*

—2 Corinthians 6:17–18

Every father desires a great future for his children. He will do everything possible to make sure his children have a better life and a good future. The Lord also has a plan and a good future for you. His plan is prosperity, not poverty. As you surrender your life to the Lord Jesus, you automatically enter the glorious destiny that has been awaiting you. Now, as a child with a great destiny and of a glorious and higher kingdom, you have to separate yourself from the world and commit your soul unto the Lord Jesus, which secures your destiny.

> For Moses had said, *Conse-crate yourselves to day to the* LORD, even every man upon his son, and upon his brother; that he may bestow upon you a blessing this day. (Exodus 32:29)

When the Lord bestows His blessing upon you based on your dedication to Him, neither the devil nor his agent can reverse it. You shouldn't be conformed to this world by following a worldly pattern. You should set your mind and affections above, and that will put you above, not beneath; you become the head, not the tail. The easiest way to shut the door to Satan and keep him from having access to your destiny and tying down your life is to follow a godly pattern instead of a worldly pattern. Those who are committed to serving the Lord place security over their life and destiny. When Satan was given permission to test Job with affliction, he went back to God to inform Him that He still had His protection over Job's life and all that pertained to Job. The Lord had to remove the divine covering over the life of Job, who was committed to Him, before Satan could afflict him with sickness and tie down everything he had.

> Then Satan answered the LORD, and said, Doth Job fear

> God for nought? Hast not thou made an hedge about him, and about his house, and about all that he hath on every side? thou hast blessed the work of his hands, and his substance is increased in the land. (Job 1:9–10)

> If thou return to the Almighty, thou shalt be built up, *Thou shalt put away iniquity far from thy tabernacles* [life]. Then shalt thou lay up gold as dust... *Yea, the Almighty shall be thy defense, And thou shalt have plenty of silver.* When men are cast down, then thou shalt say, there is lifting up. (Job 22:23–25, 29; italics added)

I know it is your desire to lay up gold as dust and have plenty of silver, which indicates prosperity, one of God's blessings of consecration. But you have a part to play. Your part is to put away iniquity to enjoy the full blessing of God. Not only will you prosper, but the Lord will be the defense of your life and prosperity. Iniquity is the greatest threat to a great destiny, ministry, etc. Many lives and destinies are being choked from having an expression because of iniquity. We have been redeemed as kings and priests and are a royal priesthood, peculiar and holy people with a great destiny for the purpose of His glory. He has separated us from darkness to walk in the light.

## Walk as light

Walking in the light brings the full blessing of God, while failure to walk in the light brings defeat and failure.

> For ye were sometimes darkness, but now are ye light in the Lord: walk as children of light. (Ephesians 5:8)

> But the path of the just is as the shining light, that shineth more and more unto the perfect day. The way of the wicked [ungodly] is as darkness: they know not at what they stumble. (Proverbs 4:18–19)

As a child of God, we are distinguished by nature because we have the life of Christ imparted into our spirit by the Holy Spirit. Unbelievers don't have the nature of Christ because they don't have the Holy Spirit. For that reason, we have to be distinguished in character by living differently from the world (unbelievers) and be an example to them in words and deeds. The number one act of evangelism is your daily lifestyle as a believer. The way you live and act is a message to those who are unsaved, whether they should accept Christ or reject Him.

> Let your light shine before
> others, that they may see your
> good deeds and glorify your
> Father in heaven. (Matthew 5:16)

Our lives should be an expression of the life of Jesus Christ.

One of my coworkers, who always used cuss words as a primary means of communication, walked up to me in the break room and said, "Abel, I notice something about you. I haven't heard you cuss."

Jokingly, I said, "If I'm cussing and you're cussing, who will tell whom not to cuss?"

He laughed. But one thing he promised was not to cuss. Even though it won't happen in one day, he's working on it.

As a young man, my friend invited me to one of his group's yearly events. While at the event, my friend and others were drinking alcohol, vaping, and doing all sorts of things. I sat on the couch until the Holy Spirit made me feel uncomfortable enough to leave the environment.

The next day, when I went to see my friend, he was mad at me. He said, "Abel, you act like you are the only holy person on earth, and you alone know God."

I replied, "No, don't think like that. I can't compromise my spiritual principles for associations."

Then I said nicely with a smile, "Moreover, since you brought that up, if I partake of those things you did at the event, who will pray for you while the devil is knocking at your door while the Lord is also knocking? I know my flesh was craving for everything at the event last night [drinking, vaping, etc.], but I had to yield to the Spirit to overcome the sinful desire of the flesh to maintain my spiritual fire for the benefit of you and others."

Caution: You have to be vigilant by being spiritual rather than being carnal because the devil roars like a lion, seeking souls to destroy. Sin gives the devil access to your mind to pollute your life. It darkens your understanding of the plan and purpose of God for your life. It is destructive. Sin places weight on your life to suppress your destiny. It has robbed many people of greatness and has brought down mighty men and ministries. It robs the anointed of the anointing, destroys marriages, and blocks the visions of visionaries.

> Let us lay aside *every weight, and the sin* which doth so easily beset us, and let us run with patience the race that is set before us. (Hebrews 12:1)

To dominate the world, which is full of gloom and darkness, you have to walk in the light because only light brightens every darkness. Live a distinguished life from the ungodly or unbelievers to prosper in whatever you do. You can't dominate darkness by walking in darkness. You can't influence an unbeliever to serve our Lord Jesus while you live like them. Do not live like the world but with the awareness that you belong to the kingdom of God, not to the kingdom of darkness. We were translated from the kingdom of darkness into the kingdom of light, so walk as a child of light. To have a shining path without stumbling blocks to your destiny, walk in the light, and every darkness will be shattered.

> Nevertheless the foundation of God standeth sure, having this seal, the Lord knoweth them that are his. And, let every one that nameth the name of Christ depart from iniquity. (2 Timothy 2:19)

> For bodily exercise profiteth little: but godliness is profitable unto all things, having promise of the life that now is, and of that which is to come. (1 Timothy 4:8)

## Fear of the Lord

Godliness will profit you more than anything else. It comes with lot of promises both in this life and the afterlife. Making the decision to put away iniquity and walk in the fear of the Lord is the best choice you can make, as it will set you on a throne just as Joseph inherited the throne in Egypt. Joseph had a destiny hovering over his life. At the age of seventeen, the Lord revealed that he was going to be great. Despite this promise, he was sold as a slave into Egypt and tempted by the wife of Potiphar to sleep with her. He feared the Lord and escaped for his destiny. Even though Potiphar's wife lied and he was wrongfully imprisoned, the Lord favored Joseph and granted him the wisdom to interpret Pharaoh's dream, which lifted him to the throne (Genesis 37, 39, 41).

Sin is pleasurable to many, but its end is destructive. When the Lord appeared to Abraham, He first introduced Himself as Almighty and gave him the command to walk before Him blamelessly or perfectly, which was followed by His promises of greatness to Abraham (Genesis 17). Jesus said, "The prince of this world [Satan] has nothing in me" (John 14:30). This means the works of darkness and sin were not found around His life and ministry. He is an example to us. Through His obedience to the will of God, He is highly exalted and given a name that is above every name. His throne and dominion are forever.

The fear of God is one of the platforms on which the promise of God is delivered. Saul lost the throne because of disobedience. Solomon failed and lost the throne because of iniquity. He began his leadership with the fear of the Lord, and the Lord told him to ask for whatever he wanted. He asked for wisdom, and it was given to him. He became one of the wisest men that ever walked this planet. The Lord added wealth and riches to his life. Samson fell to the deception of Delilah and lost his power (anointing) to conquer because of iniquity. Your destiny is great, and you don't want to yield to the pleasure of sin. Separate yourself from the world, live by biblical principles daily, and the Lord will decorate your life and honor you.

> The fear of the LORD is to hate evil…the evil way, and the froward mouth, do I hate. Counsel is mine, and sound wisdom: I am understanding; I have strength. By me kings reign, and princes decree justice. By me princes rule, and nobles, even all the judges of the earth. (Proverbs 8:13–16)

Wisdom begins with walking in the fear of the Lord. It is by this wisdom, which is walking in the fear of the Lord, that He guides the affairs of kings and rulers. Also, it is by fearing the Lord that one is exalted by the Lord to sit with the high and mighty and do great in life and ministry.

I know the question running through your mind. You may ask why an unbeliever is doing great. The devil can give you this world only if he can destroy your soul. The devil took Jesus to a high mountain, showed Him the world and its splendor, and told Him it was His for the taking if He bowed down to serve him. He's still walking about with that agenda—to divert you from the true blessing, riches, and greatness that come from God—because the blessing of God makes rich and adds no sorrow. You endanger your destiny, like King Solomon, by perpetually walking in iniquity.

> Again, the devil taketh him up into an exceeding high mountain, and sheweth him all the kingdoms of the world, and the glory of them; and saith unto him, All these things will I give thee, if thou wilt fall down and worship me. Then saith Jesus unto him, Get thee hence, Satan: for it is written, thou shalt worship the Lord thy God, and him only shalt thou serve. (Matthew 4:8–10)

> Blessed is the man that walketh not in the counsel of the ungodly, nor standeth in the way of sinners, nor sitteth in the seat of the scornful. But his delight is in the law of the Lord; and in his law doth he meditate day and

night. And he shall be like a tree planted by the rivers of water, that bringeth forth his fruit in his season; his leaf also shall not wither; *and whatsoever he doeth shall prosper.* The ungodly are not so: but are like the chaff which the wind driveth away. (Psalm 1:1–4; italics added)

Your prosperity rests on you more than God. The Lord is committed to His Word, to see it fulfilled. He said that if you consecrate or separate yourself from the world and live a life distinguished from the unbeliever, everything you do shall prosper, and nothing will go dry or empty in your life. In famine or difficulties, He will satisfy your soul. The plan of God for your life is great. Even though your beginning is small and nothing around your life or ministry seems great, the Lord guarantees you a greater ending when you stay dedicated to Him by not allowing circumstances to divert your mind from Him to walk in iniquity, which will rob you of your prosperity. Live a separate life from the ungodly because you have a great destiny over your life.

When the devil or his agents, who could be your associates, try to entice you to sin or follow sinful deeds, do not consent. You carry a generational blessing because the blessing of God is not selfish. By choosing to walk in the way of the Lord, you are not only preserving your destiny but also the destiny of those who come after you.

> Blessed is the man that feareth the LORD, that delighteth greatly in his commandments. His seed shall be mighty upon earth: the generation of the upright shall be blessed. Wealth and riches shall be in his house: and his righteousness endureth for ever. (Psalm 112:1–3)

# About the Author

Abel Jimmy was born in 1994 in Liberia and is a naturalized citizen of the United States of America. He obtained a degree in government, politics, and policy from Liberty University in Lynchburg, Virginia. He's the author of the book *Living a Triumphant Life*. While in college, he felt a pull in his spirit by the Holy Spirit to preach, which he tried to escape from.

On February 12, 2022, he went before the Lord to find out His will for his life; and at three in the morning, he heard a voice that said, "My hand is upon you." Wondering what that meant, he searched the Scriptures and found out that the phrase "My hand is upon you" refers to the spirit of the Lord.

Reflecting on why the spirit of the Lord was upon him, the Lord directed him to Luke 4:18 to confirm that He had placed in his spirit the call to preach by the enablement of the Spirit.

Since then, he has been teaching a small fellowship group online, which he started in 2022 as preparation for the ministry God has for him. He is a member of the Winners Chapel International, based in Nigeria. He considers Bishop David Oyedepo, E. A. Adeboye, and Dr. Paul Enenche as his mentors.